I Can, Kim Can

Written by Greg Cook

Illustrated by Karin Littlewood

Collins

I can get a top on.

Kim cannot.

I can get socks on.

Kim cannot. Mum can.

I can tip it in.

Kim cannot. Kim tips the cup.

I can pack up the pens.

Kim cannot. Kim tips the pot.

I can kick it in the net.

Kim cannot kick.

Kim can pick it up.

I can pick Kim up!

I can

Kim cannot

Ideas for reading

Linda Pagett B.Ed(Hons), M.Ed
Lecturer and Educational Consultant

Learning objectives: read simple words by sounding out and blending the phonemes all through the word from left to right; explore and experiment with sounds, words and texts; use phonic knowledge to write simple regular words; hear and say sounds in words in the order in which they occur; recognise common digraphs

Curriculum links: Understanding the World: People and communities

Focus phonemes: c, a, n, k, i, m, ck, n, o, t

Fast words: I, the

Word count: 60

Getting started

- Read the title and draw children's attention to the comma in the title. Demonstrate how to read it with a short pause.

- Look at the cover and discuss the age of the characters. Ask children if they have younger brothers and sisters, and discuss what they can and cannot do and why.

- Read aloud the blurb on the back cover together. Model how to sound out the word *k-i-ck*, and to blend the phoneme to read the word.

- Using magnetic letters, spell together *c-a-n* sounding out each phoneme. Make new words by changing the first consonant, e.g. fan, man, pan, practising segmenting and blending.

Reading and responding

- Read pp2–5 and challenge children to add sound buttons to the word *c-a-n-n-o-t* and to practise blending the sounds to read the word fluently.

- Ask children to read to p13 aloud, praising them for recognising whole words and sounding out those they are unsure of.

- Support children as they decode longer words with focus phonemes, e.g. sock, pack, kick, pick.